TABLE OF CONTENTS

Introduction to Zoom

Zoom is now the video communication platform of choice for federal governments, tech startups, religious communities, and, of course, regular people looking to chat and even party with their friends and family. Here's everything you need to know about Zoom, including how to download it and get started, along with a few tips and tricks to help you become a video-chatting pro.

Zoom's story dates back to 2011, a time when the market for video conferencing software was crowded, as businesses searched for a more convenient way to communicate face-to-face. Delivering an alternative solution to the complicated and often expensive video strategies of the day, Zoom was a breath of fresh are too many companies.

Zoom proved that modern companies could communicate through video just as naturally as through audio and chat – and they could do it without the glitches of previous solutions. Zoom Meetings became the core product of the portfolio, delivering an incredible combination of HD video and audio, as well as things like transcripts of calls and intelligent features too.

To make the Zoom solution even more impressive, the company even implemented it's own free tier, so that team members can start connecting without paying anything at all. Today, you can access Zoom for everything from online webinars and training sessions, to state-of-the-art calls and even instant chat. Let's take a closer look.

What Is Zoom?

Zoom is a cloud-based video communications app that allows you to set up virtual video and audio conferencing, webinars, live chats, screen-sharing, and other collaborative capabilities.

You don't need an account to attend a Zoom meeting, and the platform is compatible with Mac, Windows, Linux, iOS, and Android, meaning nearly anyone can access it. Of course, video conferencing apps aren't new. Zoom is just one in a long line of communication tools that include Skype, Cisco Webex, and Google Meet, among others.

In short, a big part of Zoom's appeal is simplicity. It's easy to get started, the app is lightweight, and the interface is relatively intuitive to use with popular features like Gallery View a mode that allows you to see every person on the call at once built right into the app.

Tips And Tricks

If you're looking to get more out of Zoom, you may be interested in a few more settings and features. Beyond simple tricks like knowing how to mute yourself and others on the call, you should familiarize yourself with the platforms advanced settings:

- ❖ One of the platform's more lively features, virtual background allows you to display and image or video as your background.
- ❖ A helpful feature that allows you to take control of another participant's screen.
- ❖ Only available for Pro accounts or higher, a Personal Meeting ID will make your meetings more secure, while also making it easier for your friends and colleagues to connect.

- A feature that lets you control when participants join a meeting.

Zoom Rooms

If you're subscribed to the Pro pricing plan or higher, you gain access to Zoom Rooms, the company's conference room software, and hardware that can turn any room into an official conference room. For $49 a month, you gain access to the Zoom Room software. This software connects a television or monitor with your computer, an external camera, and a microphone. Put together, you can turn nearly any room into a professional-grade conference room. If you're looking to make your business as Zoom-friendly as possible, Zoom Rooms are a worthwhile investment.

What Is Zoombombing?

You might have heard the term "Zoombombing" before. This refers to people who gain access to Zoom calls without being invited and try to wreak havoc. Earlier in the year, there were several widely reported Zoombombing cases, which led the company to crack down on them. Now, whenever you start a call, it'll be password-protected by default, making it exponentially harder for anyone you don't know to gain access. Most calls also have a "waiting room" function, which requires the host to approve anyone who wants access to the call.

Chapter 1: What Is Zoom?

What Is Zoom?

Zoom is a cloud-based video conferencing service you can use to virtually meet with others - either by video or audio-only or both, all while conducting live chats - and it lets you record those sessions to view later.

In a world defined by remote working and globalization, the video provides businesses with a way to maintain face-to-face interactions between disparate members of staff. Video can bring more context and meaning to a meeting while improving daily interactions. It's no wonder, then, that one of the most popular and valuable companies in the communications industry today is a brand that started its ascent to fame with video conferencing.

Zoom is best-known for being the go-to choice for businesses that need access to quick and convenient videos for internal and external conferencing. The company made the headlines with its public debut, breaking records for soaring business value. Today, Zoom is continuing to build out it's collaborative offering, implementing new tools, new security measures, and various other updates to serve the changing marketplace.

When people are talking about Zoom, you'll usually hear the following phrases: Zoom Meeting and Zoom Room. A-Zoom Meeting refers to a video conferencing meeting that's hosted using Zoom. You can join these meetings via a webcam or phone. Meanwhile, a Zoom Room is the physical hardware setup that lets companies schedule and launches Zoom Meetings from their conference rooms. Zoom Rooms require an additional subscription on top of a Zoom subscription and are an ideal solution for larger companies.

Zoom's Main Features

Here Are Zoom's Core Features:

1. **One-On-One Meetings:** Host unlimited one-on-one meetings even with the free plan.

2. **Group Video Conferences:** Host up to 500 participants (if you purchase the "large meeting" add-on). The free plan, however, allows you to host video conferences of up to 40 minutes and up to 100 participants.

3. **Screen Sharing:** Meet one-on-one or with large groups and share your screen with them so they can see what you see.

Zoom Meetings Review: Features

At all price levels, Zoom delivers everything you need for sensational video conferencing. The video quality that you get is excellent, and audio comes through too. You can share multiple screens and use whiteboard functions to annotate projects. Additionally, Zoom gives you the freedom to connect on any device that suits you including your smartphone. Some of the most exciting features of Zoom Meetings include:

- ❖ Easy adoption with WebRTC technology
- ❖ Join from anywhere on any device
- ❖ Access robust security solutions throughout
- ❖ Built-in tools for screen sharing
- ❖ HD video and audio calls
- ❖ Support for up to 1,000 video participants and 49 videos

- ❖ Meet securely with role-based user permissions
- ❖ Streamlined calendaring services with Outlook and Google
- ❖ Built-in recording and transcripts
- ❖ Team chat both for groups and one-on-one messaging
- ❖ Access to extra features like webinars, chat, and phone

Zoom Meetings Review: Benefits

Perhaps the biggest benefit of Zoom is how accessible the technology is. Setting up a Zoom Meeting is as simple as clicking on an invitation link to launch the app or prompt users to install the interface. There's no need for any mass provisioning solutions, and the interface is lightweight and straightforward on both mobile and desktop devices. Of course, there's more to Zoom than just simplicity. Zoom also offers super-fast functionality, with high-quality audio and video at every price-point.

Other Benefits Include:

Security: Although security has been a point of contention for Zoom, specifically during the COVID-19 pandemic, the company has committed to improving this factor. Zoom is making important changes to its security strategy and implementing new features. For instance, all meetings now require host permission and a password to join

1. Excellent Support: Zoom boasts fantastic user support to serve companies around the world. There's phone support available through multiple time zones. You can get a quick answer to your questions whenever you need them. However, the solution is so easy to use that you shouldn't have too much trouble

2. Scheduling: You can also schedule meetings in advance from your Zoom app, which you can connect to a range of other

calendars, including those from Google and Microsoft. This makes it easier to get everyone connected using the tools you love

3. Advanced Features: Another benefit of Zoom is that it's constantly updating and improving what you can do with the technology. Virtual backgrounds allow you to get rid of the messy meeting room in the background of your call. Additionally, there are even touch-up functionalities too for those who are worried about wrinkles

Immersive Host Controls: The host controls in Zoom provide excellent control over how your meeting runs. You can create a co-host for your meetings if you're working with another consultant. Additionally, there's access to desktop sharing and hand-over controls too

Excellent Engagement: As well as delivering a futuristic and straightforward experience, Zoom also makes it easy to keep your team engaged with things like virtual hand-raising and other exciting functionalities

Zoom App Downloads

The desktop app is available for Windows and macOS, while the mobile app is available for Android and iOS. All the apps let you join a meeting without signing in, but also let you sign in using a Zoom account, Google, Facebook, or SSO. From there, you can start a meeting, join a meeting, share your screen in a Zoom Room by entering the meeting ID, start Zoom Meetings, mute/unmute your mic, start/stop the video, invite others to the meeting, change your screen name, do in-meeting chat, and start a cloud recording. If you're a desktop user, you can also start a local recording, create polls, broadcast your Facebook live on Facebook, and more. In other words, the desktop app is more fully-featured, although, if you're a free user, you can still get a lot of mileage from the mobile app.

Zoom Outlook Plugin

As well as the various other Zoom app downloads, it is also possible to use Zoom in other ways. For example, there's a Zoom Outlook plugin that's designed to work directly in your Microsoft Outlook client or as an Add-in for Outlook on the web. This Outlook plug drops a Zoom button right into the standard Outlook toolbar and lets you start or schedule a Zoom meeting with a simple click.

Zoom Browser Extensions

Another tool for quickly starting or scheduling a Zoom meeting comes in the form of an extension for your favorite browser. There are a Zoom Chrome extension and Zoom Firefox add-on that let you schedule a Zoom meeting via Google Calendar. A simple click on the Zoom button and you can start a meeting or schedule one for later with all the information on the meeting being sent via Google Calendar to make it easy for participants to join.

Zoom Meetings Review: Add-Ons And Extras

One of the things that makes Zoom such a compelling choice for those in search of collaborative tools is that it's incredibly flexible. Zoom allows businesses to connect their Zoom functionality to a wide range of apps and online services, including Microsoft Teams, Slack, and countless other tools. You can even access the Workplace by Facebook, and Google Calendar.

Thanks to open API access, it's easy to implement features from Zoom into your existing environment, too if you have the technical know-how. Aside from a range of integrations, Zoom also provides a range of "add-ons" to support today's teams, including:

Zoom Rooms

Zoom Rooms are the hardware and software solutions from Zoom designed to help businesses create accessible meeting rooms. You can access one-touch meeting starts, HD audio and video, and all of the latest technology from Zoom in a huddle-room ready package. Building the perfect conference room is easy with Zoom Rooms, and you can even access a range of different hardware options to suit your preferences. Features include:

❖ Conference room connectors so you can use your existing hardware
❖ HD video and audio access
❖ One-touch meeting join
❖ Powerful security built-in
❖ One-click wireless sharing
❖ Co-annotation whiteboards
❖ Range of options for rooms of all sizes
❖ Scheduling displays
❖ Remote management and software provisioning
❖ Room and location hierarchies
❖ Role-based administration

Zoom Webinars

Zoom Video Webinars allow you to host events with up to 100 interactive participants who you can interact with, and 1,000 view-only attendees. Like other Zoom solutions, webinars are easy to set up with branded emails and registration forms available. There are multiple integrations for your CRM systems too. Features include everything from live broadcasting to event assistance from Zoom specialists, and even reporting and analytics. You also get on-demand viewing solutions, with auto-generated transcripts. Features include:

- ❖ Auto-generated transcripts
- ❖ On-demand or recurring webinars
- ❖ HD video and audio for up to 100 panelists
- ❖ Reporting and analytics on attendees and engagement
- ❖ Live broadcasts via social channels and YouTube
- ❖ Event assistance from the Zoom Team
- ❖ Host controls like mute/unmute and more
- ❖ Q&A and polling features
- ❖ Hand-raising
- ❖ Instant chat for attendees and presenters

Zoom Chat

Zoom Chat is included with your Zoom Meetings license. Designed to keep teams connected, Chat ensures that you can streamline your teams with a quick instant messaging, and integrations with all your favorite tools. An intelligent search is built-in, and you can choose between one-on-one and group chat too. Starred channels and contacts make it easy to stay focused, while status and presence features show you who is online. There's even security and archiving for compliance purposes. Features include:

- ❖ Instant one-on-one or group chat
- ❖ Status and presence indicators
- ❖ Tools for productivity
- ❖ Archiving and security with multi-factor authentication
- ❖ Quick search functionality
- ❖ Calendar integrations
- ❖ Mobile and desktop access
- ❖ Settings and notifications to help control the feed

Zoom Phone

Zoom Phone is the enterprise cloud phone system from Zoom, providing businesses with an all-in-one environment for business voice and collaboration. You can access the features of a traditional phone features, including centralized provisioning and management, as well as auto-attendants and HD calling. Other features include:

* ❖ Intelligent call routing and auto attendants
* ❖ Integrations with Microsoft, Salesforce, and Google
* ❖ Voicemail and call recordings
* ❖ Bring your carrier functionality
* ❖ Secure HD audio
* ❖ Standards-based endpoints interoperability
* ❖ One-touch meeting or call join
* ❖ An accelerated path to the cloud
* ❖ Dashboards to monitor call health

Transforming The State Of Video Collaboration

Zoom might have started as the go-to solution for simple video conversations, but it's a lot more than that today. Although the company still excels at keeping teams and external contractors connected with quick and easy access points, it can also accomplish a lot more. Depending on your needs, you could build your entire communication and collaboration stack within Zoom, tapping into everything from Zoom Chat, to Zoom Phone for traditional business voice features.

The Zoom environment continues to expand and evolve to suit the needs of its audience today. As the world continues to embrace the potential of remote work, Zoom is rapidly becoming an all-in-one solution for productivity and efficiency in this new environment. Today's workplace leaders can take advantage of Zoom for chat, video, and audio alike.

Although Zoom has had a few issues with things like security and rapid scaling in the past, the company is improving all of the time. The brand has responded to concerns about security and is working harder to ensure that its full-stack offering is as appealing to enterprises as possible.

Recording Zoom Meetings On Mobile

It is possible to record Zoom meetings and calls on mobile too. However, this is done via cloud recordings so you need a paid Zoom membership to use this feature. It's also worth noting that cloud storage is limited, so be careful how many meetings you record while using the mobile app.

To Record A Zoom Call On Mobile Follow These Steps:

- ❖ Open the Zoom app on your mobile
- ❖ Click to join or start a meeting
- ❖ Click the three-dot menu on the bottom right of the screen
- ❖ Click "Record to the cloud" or "record"
- ❖ You'll then see a recording icon and the ability to pause or stop recording
- ❖ Once the call is over you'll find the recording in the "My Recordings" section of the Zoom site

Where Does Zoom Save Recordings?

When you're recording locally, Zoom call recordings are saved on the Zoom folder on your PC or Mac. These can be found at these locations:

- ❖ PC: C:\Users\User Name\Documents\Zoom
- ❖ Mac: /Users/User Name/Documents/Zoom

You can easily access Zoom recordings by opening the Zoom app and navigating to meetings. Once there you'll see a "recorded" tab where you can choose the meeting you need then either play the recording or open it. For cloud storage of your Zoom meeting recordings log in to your account and navigate to the My Recordings page.

Zoom Screen Sharing And Using Pause Share

Did you know that you can not only share your screen (smartphone and desktop) but also pause your screen sharing? Simply press Pause Share when you don't want your meeting participants to watch you mess around your presentation slides.

Share And Annotate On Mobile

You can share files directly from your phone while in the meeting and use the whiteboarding feature on your phone by writing comments with your finger. To annotate while viewing someone else's shared screen, select View Options from the top of the Zoom window, and then choose Annotate. A toolbar will appear with all your options for annotating - such as text, draw, arrow, and so on.

Zoom Keyboard Shortcut

It's possible to use various shortcut keys during Zoom meetings to access features or change settings easily. These include a multitude of things but our favorites are:

- ❖ Alt + A or Command(⌘)+Shift+A: Mute/unmute audio
- ❖ Alt+M or Command(⌘)+Control+M: Mute/unmute audio for everyone except the host
- ❖ Alt+S or Command(⌘)+Control+S: Start screen sharing
- ❖ Alt+R or Command(⌘)+Shift+R: Start/stop local recording

- ❖ Alt+C or Command(⌘)+Shift+C: Start/stop cloud recording
- ❖ Alt+P or Command(⌘)+Shift+P: Pause or resume recording
- ❖ Alt+F1 or Command(⌘)+Shift+W: Switch to active speaker view in video meeting

Add Filters To Your Zoom Calls

As well as virtual backgrounds, it's possible to jazz up your Zoom calls by using filters. These come in two forms and can be found in the same background settings as virtual backgrounds. You can choose either add simple color shades to your camera (sepia, black and white, and such) or select from several Snapchat- filters to add cartoon stylings to your camera. These might not be ideal for business calls but should make things more entertaining with friends and family.

Touch Up My Appearance

As well as virtual backgrounds, Zoom offers the ability to improve your looks when you're on a call. There's a feature called "Touch Up My Appearance" which is useful if you've not had your daily caffeine fix or are struggling with life in the home office. Touch Up My Appearance uses a filter to subtly smooth fine lines and it's meant to look very natural. To use Touch Up My Appearance, go to Settings, and under the Video tab, check the box next to Touch up.

Recording Transcripts

As well as recording Zoom meetings, you can also automatically transcribe the audio of a meeting that you record to the cloud. And, as the meeting host, you can edit your transcript, scan the transcript text for keywords to access the video at that moment, and share the recording. To enable the Audio Transcript feature for your use, sign into the Zoom web portal and navigate to My Meeting Settings, then go to the Cloud recording option on the Recording tab, and verify that the setting is enabled. Choose Turn On, if need be. If the option is greyed out, it has been locked at either the Group or Account level, and you will need to contact your Zoom admin.

Zoom Virtual Backgrounds

If you want to jazz things up a bit or don't want other people on the Zoom call seeing the awful mess of your home then there's good news as Zoom offers virtual backgrounds. These are backdrops for your calls that include things like space, cityscapes, and ocean-side views too. With Zoom virtual backgrounds, you can also upload an image of anything you want to customize your background. It's available for both iPhone and desktops

How To Use Virtual Backgrounds On Desktop

It's fairly easy to get started with Zoom virtual backgrounds. On a Mac or PC, for instance, just open up your Zoom client, click on the "Setup" icon on the corner, and select "Virtual Background" in the side menu. Zoom provides a few virtual backgrounds. Click on the one you'd like to use. If you would like your background, click on the plus sign above and to the left of the sample backgrounds, choose an image from your computer, and add it.

You can also add a virtual background during a meeting. In your Zoom client, click on the arrow next to the video symbol on the left, select "Choose a virtual background...", and you will see the same Virtual Background page. The company recommends using a green screen and a good webcam to get the best results, but it is possible to use a virtual background without a green screen too.

How To Use Virtual Backgrounds On The Mobile App

You can use Zoom virtual backgrounds on the app too. Login to your account and joining a meeting via your phone. Then click the three dots at the bottom of the screen and click the "more" menu. Then click "virtual background" and choose the background you want to use.

Removing Background Noise From Your Zoom Calls

Zoom has introduced settings that allow you to adjust the audio on your call and remove unnecessary and unwanted background noise. To activate this, click into the settings, then find the audio options. In there you'll see a drop-down menu with "suppress background noise". There are varying levels of suppression you can add here. The highest will remove as much as possible, reducing issues with fan noises and dogs barking while the lower levels will still let you play background music on a chilled-out casual call with friends. If the built-in noise removal isn't enough there are other options available.

How To Improve Your Microphone quality With AI

If you don't have a perfectly peaceful office to work from then you might find things are a bit noisy and less than professional for your calls. Nvidia has the solution with an AI-powered piece of software that can eliminate background noise from your calls. You need to be running Windows 10 and have Nvidia GeForce RTX or Quadro RTX graphics card but if you tick those boxes you can use Nvidia RTX Voice to remove unwanted noise from your microphone. I've written a detailed guide on how to setup RTX Voice here, but essentially you just need to download the software, then set it as your default input and output device within the app:

❖ Once you've done that, you should then find the quality of your microphone is improved and your meetings are much more professional.

Security Challenge: Zoombombings

A significant number of the so-called Zoom bombings - the practice of hijacking video conversations by uninvited parties to disrupt the usual proceedings - were reported since the global quarantine began. Hijackers, who can be anyone from school children spreading hateful comments or threats, to adults spreading racist content or even porn, have given rise to a new kind of internet trolling. IT Security Administrators must be wary of this phenomenon and implement stringent policies to prevent such attacks.

Security Challenge: Data Leakages

It has been reported that attackers can use the Zoom Windows client's group chat feature to share links that will leak the Windows network credentials of anyone who clicks on them. It happens because the Zoom client converts Windows networking Universal Naming Convention (UNC) paths into clickable links. When someone clicks on that link, Windows shares the user's login credentials. This is usually a consequence of unwarranted logins to the enterprise cloud architecture, so keeping strong password policies is crucial, just as knowing about every instance of UNC path sharing.

Security Challenge: Privacy Shortcomings

According to Business Insider, Zoom has been accused of passing on data to third parties, including Facebook, without notifying the users. Vice reported that the iOS version of Zoom's app sends analytics to Facebook even for users who don't have a Facebook account, attacking the privacy of its users.

Performance Challenge: Ensuring Quality Of Service

Zoom offers best-in-class performance. Nonetheless, in areas with poor reception or the strained WiFi networks at home, its quality of meetings may downgrade. IT Administrators may find it challenging to monitor whether the tool is performing as expected for their employees.

Reliability Challenge: Ensuring Availability At All Times

When your employees rely on a single tool to plan, collaborate, and make decisions, a single disruption can negatively impact the overall schedule. IT Administrators must be notified in advance when Zoom is unavailable or not performing as expected, so they could in turn inform their employees to use alternate collaboration software.

Chapter 2: How does Zoom Work

Zoom is a web-based video conferencing tool with a local, desktop client and a mobile app that allows users to meet online, with or without video. Zoom users can choose to record sessions, collaborate on projects, and share or annotate on one another's screens, all with one easy-to-use platform. Zoom offers quality video, audio, and a wireless screen-sharing performance across windows, Mac, Linux, iOS, Android, Blackberry, Zoom Rooms, and H.323/SIP room systems.

How Does It Work?

Joining A Meeting

- ❖ Go to Zoom.us
- ❖ Click the "Join a Meeting" tab. You can find the tab on the top right corner of the homepage
- ❖ When prompted, add your designated Meeting ID (The Meeting ID can be a 9, 10, or 11-Digit number). The Meeting ID should be provided by the host.
- ❖ You're in!

Start A Meeting

- ❖ Go to Zoom.us
- ❖ Toggle over the "Host a Meeting" tab on the top right-hand corner
- ❖ Choose whether you would like to keep video chat on or off

- ❖ Sign in using your login information or create a new account
- ❖ Launch the Zoom application and open
- ❖ Send out the meeting details, including the Meeting ID and/or link
- ❖ You've created a meeting!

Sharing Your Screen

1. Zoom allows users to share their screen to the entire conference call! To do so, simply click "Share Screen" at the bottom of the window.

Note: Only one person can use screen-share at a time, and one person must "Stop Sharing" before someone else can start sharing.

2. To stop sharing the screen, simply click "Stop Sharing."

How Does Zoom Work?

Choose Your Plan

Zoom allows one-to-one chat sessions that can grow into group calls, training sessions, and webinars for internal and external audiences, and global video meetings with up to 1,000 participants and as many as 49 on-screen videos. The free tier allows unlimited one-on-one meetings but limits group sessions to 40 minutes and 100 participants. Paid plans start at $15 per month per host.

Zoom Offers Four Pricing Tiers (Not Including A Zoom Room Subscription):

1. Zoom Free: This tier is free. You can hold an unlimited number of meetings. Group meetings with multiple participants are capped at 40 minutes in length, and meetings can't be recorded.

2. Zoom Pro: This tier costs $14.99/£11.99 per month and meeting host. It allows hosts to create personal meeting IDs for repetitive Zoom Meetings, and it allows meeting recording in the cloud or your device, but it caps group meeting durations at 24 hours.

3. Zoom Business: This tier costs $19.99/£15.99 per month and meeting host (10 minimum). It lets you brand Zoom meetings with vanity URLs and company branding, and it offers transcripts of Zoom meetings recorded in the cloud, as well as dedicated customer support.

4. Zoom Enterprise: This tier costs $19.99/£15.99 per month and per meeting host (100 minimum) and is meant for businesses with 1,000+ employees. It offers unlimited cloud storage for recordings, a customer success manager, and discounts on webinars and Zoom Rooms.

5. Optional - Zoom Rooms: If you want to set up Zoom Rooms, you can sign up for a free 30-day trial, after which Zoom Rooms require an additional $49/£39 per month and room subscription, while webinars using Zoom cost $40/£32 per month and host.

How To Get Zoom

Before we go any further, it's important to note that the platform offers four distinct pricing plans, from Basic to Enterprise. What's right for you depends on how you plan to use the app:

Zoom Basic: This is the platform's most popular pricing tier, which makes sense, considering that it's free. This tier offers unlimited one-on-one meetings, but video conferencing with more than three participants is limited to 40 minutes (you can always start another one). If you plan to use it only every once in a while to chat with friends or family, check out our general overview of Zoom's basic features.

Zoom Pro: The Pro plan is ideal if you work with a small team or plan to regularly conduct extended video calls. Beyond extending the group meeting length from 40 minutes to 24 hours, this tier allows hosts to create IDs for recurring meetings and the capability to store recorded meetings in the cloud, plus advanced usage reports.

Zoom Business: A pricing plan to make collaboration easy for small to medium-sized companies, the Business tier requires at least 10 hosts. But what you get in return is company branding on all invites, dedicated customer support, and more features like auto-generated transcription.

Zoom Enterprise: This tier is designed for large businesses and sign-up requires a minimum of at least 100 hosts. Enterprise offers plenty of perks, including unlimited cloud storage, a dedicated "customer success manager" and the capacity to host 500 people on a single call.

Pros

Reimagining Online Video Conferencing: Imagine if Skype was on steroids. Using HD video and voice, Zoom brings innovation into meetings and webinars. Zoom also features dynamic voice detection and a choice of either full-screen, gallery view, or both using dual streaming for those of you with twice the amount of screens. If you're more laid back, you're allowed to join as a view-only attendee, or by telephone dial-in when you're on the go.

Mobile-Friendly: Zoom has a feature-rich, mobile app for both iOS and Android, allowing you to virtually connect from anywhere with an Internet connection

A Group That Zooms Together, Stays Together: Zoom makes group collaboration easier! Aside from being compatible with Mac, Windows, Linux, iOS, and Android, the program has group and private chat capabilities with screen sharing from phones, tablets, laptops, or desktop computers. Zoom allows you to annotate and co-annotate shared documents as well as gain control of the keyboard, mouse, and even the whiteboard.

Meetings At Your Convenience: You have the option of either starting an instant meeting or creating a scheduled meeting. When you schedule a meeting, a Personal Meeting ID will be assigned for you to share or distribute. As a host, you have special privileges to record a meeting or mute participants. Zoom allows you to create MP4 and M4A recordings throughout a meeting and offers Google Chrome and Outlook plug-ins. Rest assured that whatever you share, whether through a desktop or the mobile application, is at its highest quality. You can even enable optimization and sound transfer for video sharing. Aside from all this, participants have the option of virtually raising their hands for permission to ask a question or speak to a group. And using the Zoom meeting format's breakout groups, hosts can designate times for small group collaboration without ending or restarting a meeting.

Safety Is A Priority: Aside from being given your private login username and password, Zoom also implements both Secure Socket Layer (SSL) encryption and AES 256-bits encryption. Zoom features role-based access control and admin feature controls.

It's Free! That right, you don't pay anything. But of course, you have the option to pay and upgrade to gain access to even more features that Zoom offers Unlimited Number of Meetings. While using the free version, you can have as many sessions as you would like!

Cons

- ❖ When using Zoom's free plan, there is a meeting duration cap of 40 minutes. This is, of course, upgradable using a paid version.

- ❖ Also with Zoom's free plan, there is a maximum of 50 participants allowed per session. Again, this feature is upgradable using the Pro version.

Chapter 3: Difference Between Free Zoom and Paid App

What's The Difference Between Paid And Free Zoom?

There are a few differences between the paid and free Zoom plans that are worth noting.

Free Users

You can download the Zoom app on your computer or phone and join any meeting with a supplied meeting ID. You can choose to disable audio or video before joining, too. You could even create your free Zoom account, like by linking your Google account, and from there you can create a new meeting, schedule one, join a meeting, share a screen, add contacts, and so on. Just keep in mind you can only be signed in to Zoom on one computer, one tablet, and one phone at a time. If you sign in to an additional device while logged into another device of the same type, Zoom said you will be logged out automatically on the first device.

Paid Users

You can sign up and download Zoom onto your computer using your work email if your system administrator has a Pro, Business, or Enterprise account. You'll then want to sync Zoom to your calendar so you can schedule Zoom meetings and invite remote participants to join. If you're setting up a Zoom Room, you'll need a computer to sync and run Zoom Meetings and a tablet for attendees to launch the Zoom Meetings. You'll also need a mic, camera, and speaker, at least one HDTV monitors to display remote meeting participants, and an HDMI cable to share computer screens on a display, as well as an internet cable for your connection You'll also need to download "Zoom Rooms for Conference Room" on the in-room computer and "Zoom Room Controller" for the tablet in the meeting room. You can then sync those rooms to your company's shared calendar so employees can see which meeting rooms are available.

Zoom Pricing Plans Comparison

Setting up a Zoom account is fairly easy, and Zoom offers a free plan that suits a lot of people's needs, particularly those using it for personal reasons. However, for those who need more time or participants or want to add customizations to their Zoom meetings there are paid plans that offer these options.

Zoom Basic

The free version of Zoom known as Zoom Basic is a great way to test the waters if you're new to the video conferencing platform. It lets you host meetings as long as 40 minutes for up to 100 participants using HD video and HD voice. In your Zoom meetings, you're able to use virtual backgrounds to camouflage your surroundings. You can also share your screen, present to the attendees, and use whiteboarding features. Plus, you can set up a personal meeting ID and a password to protect your meetings from uninvited guests.

Also, the Basic plan allows you to create breakout rooms. These breakout rooms can be useful if a couple of team members need to have a quick discussion outside of the meeting. The Basic plan also includes the capability to record meetings.

Zoom Pro

Geared toward small teams, Zoom Pro picks up where Zoom Basic leaves off. Your meeting can last 24 hours, although you're still limited to 100 participants. But you also can manage users and grant administrative privileges, as well as generate reports like tracking how many meetings you're holding and how long they last.

Administrative and owner privileges, which you can set with a Pro plan, let you manage the account and turn features like recording, encryption and chat on and off as needed. You can also assign someone to schedule meetings for you. Zoom Pro includes 1 GB of MP4 or M4A cloud recording, which can be useful if you want to share the recording with people who couldn't make it to your meeting.

Pricing for Zoom Pro starts at $14.99 per month, per host, with a maximum of nine hosts. You can purchase the Large Meeting add-on to include more participants in your meetings. This add-on starts at $50 per month, per host for 500 participants (for a total cost of $64.99 per month, per host).

Zoom Business

For small and medium businesses, Zoom offers a plan that includes all Pro and Basic features as well as a few more. Zoom Business lets you host up to 300 participants in your meetings and allows you to customize your meeting rooms further. For example, you can use a vanity URL and add your company branding to your portals.

Additionally, Zoom Business gives you the option to deploy Zoom on-premises in your private cloud service. It also provides cloud recording transcripts, integration with learning platforms, and dedicated phone support. Zoom Business starts at $19.99 per month, per host, with a minimum of 10 hosts. The Large Meeting add-on starts at $50 per month, per host (for a total cost of $69.99 per month, per host).

Zoom Enterprise

Large enterprises can use Zoom for video conferencing, too. The Zoom Enterprise plan is designed for big companies, and meeting rooms can hold up to 500 participants. Enterprise plan subscribers can also leverage unlimited cloud storage and a dedicated customer service manager.

Zoom Enterprise includes a feature called Executive Business Reviews, which lets you analyze the adoption of the service and track ROI as well as get insight into the product roadmap for Zoom. Pricing starts at $19.99 per month, per host, with a minimum of 100 hosts. The Large Meeting Add-on starts at $50 per month, per host (for a total cost of $69.99 per month, per host).

Zoom For Education

Zoom offers a product just for educational institutions Zoom for Education. The plans start at 20 hosts and allow for up to 300 participants in a meeting. Hosts can have unlimited meetings. Features include content sharing, digital whiteboarding, integration with learning management systems, and session recording and transcription. Zoom for Education is billed on an annual basis starting at $1,800 per year. The Large Meeting add-on is $50 per month, per host.

Zoom For Healthcare

Healthcare professionals can use Zoom as well. Zoom for Healthcare provides video conferencing services that comply with the Health Insurance Portability and Accountability Act (HIPAA). This plan allows for 10 hosts and comes with a signed business associate agreement (BAA), which protects healthcare professionals if there is a data breach on Zoom's end.

Zoom for Healthcare includes collaboration features to annotate records when meeting with other doctors as well as the ability to launch a conference directly from the Epic electronic health records (EHR) system. Each session can be recorded, but clinical applications like patient visits won't be stored in the cloud.

Pricing Starts At $200 Per Month, Per Account.

When you're ready to move from a free account to a paid account, Zoom has an array of options. The different packages are clearly defined and offer the flexibility to make Zoom work for your business regardless of its size.

Chapter 4: Zoom for Teachers

Zoom Online Teaching – How To Use Zoom To Teach

How To Schedule A Zoom Meeting For An Online Class

1. Open the Zoom Desktop app on your computer

2. Click "Home" at the top left

3. Click "Schedule"

4. Enter all relevant details like time, date, topic, etc.

5. Pick your online calendar of choice (Google Calendar is great if you have Gmail or a Google account) and you'll be taken to a page with your Zoom link. You can send this link to your students in your online calendar's meeting scheduler.

How To Share Your Screen

Screen sharing is really important for presenting to your class. This button allows you to share your computer screen with everyone on the Zoom meeting. Screen sharing is very easy with Zoom, all you need to do is click the green "Share Screen" button at the bottom during your meeting. Then you'll click which screen you'd like to share (the top left one is what you'll most likely use).

Zoom Session Preparation

Before the session, make sure that you have:

❖ An internet-connected computer

- ❖ Headphones with microphone (to avoid audio feedback)
- ❖ Webcam (if you wish to be seen by others)
- ❖ A quiet space to hold the session
- ❖ A detailed session plan including timings and moderator roles
- ❖ Resources you wish to use or share, i.e. PowerPoint presentations
- ❖ Accessibility requirements of participants
- ❖ Arranged a co-presenter to moderate the chat area and answer participant questions during the session, if required (recommended for large classes)
- ❖ Scheduled your Zoom session
- ❖ Set and send any etiquette and session instruction information to participants
- ❖ Sent instructions to co-presenters or guest speakers (if applicable)
- ❖ Practiced using Zoom features in advance
- ❖ Prepared a Welcome message slide with the session start time and participant instructions to display

Ensure Participants Have:

- ❖ An internet-connected computer or mobile phone
- ❖ Session date and time
- ❖ Informed you of any accessibility needs (encourage students to inform you by a certain date to ensure you can make appropriate arrangements in time)
- ❖ Joining instructions, i.e. the participation Zoom link
- ❖ Etiquette and session guidelines for the session
- ❖ At least 30 minutes before the session
- ❖ Load your presentation and any resources to your computer ready for use.
- ❖ Clear your screen.

Tip: You should clear your screen of applications / private documents and anything else not needed for the sessions (especially important if sharing your screen)

- ❖ Join the session at least 20 minutes before the scheduled start time to run your setting checks to ensure your microphone, video, and audio work. You will be prompted to check these when you first join the session.

Tip: mute your audio/mic before until you start the session, in particular, if participants are allowed to join earlier.

- ❖ Check you have given co-host rights to your co-presenter and/or a guest speaker.
- ❖ Display the Welcome message slide with the session start time and participant
- ❖ instructions to check their settings and equipment as they join.

At The Start Of The Session

- ❖ Allow 5 minutes for late arrivals and for attendees to settle in
- ❖ Greet participants as they join the session via text chat or audio
- ❖ Remind participants to test their microphone and speakers
- ❖ Give a brief overview of the Zoom tool and how to use it during the session, including using chat and icons (i.e. raise hand)
- ❖ Remind participants the session will be recorded (if applicable) and that the recording may be viewed by students/people who have not taken part in the session (if applicable)
- ❖ Start recording (if applicable)

* Guide participants throughout the session and remind them how they can interact and locate features on the Zoom interface.

End Of The Session

* End the recording
* Save a copy of the chat (if required)

After The Session

* Session capture – Remind students that session recordings are available and where to find them (if applicable).
* Teaching with zoom

Starting A Class

* If it's your first time using Zoom, visit the Educating Guide: Getting Started on Zoom and complete the steps in advance of your class to get you set up.

* Schedule your class in the Zoom application for your desired date/time and copy the invitation details to send to your students. *Please note that students will not need to register for an account to join.

* Join your class a couple of minutes early to ensure a proper connection then follow the below tips for a quality online learning experience.

Tips And Tricks For Virtual Lessons

* For your first class, set aside some time to introduce your students to Zoom and ensure that they're able to connect their audio and video.

- ❖ Give an agenda or plan for each class by Screen Sharing a document or slide at the beginning of class. This gives students a clear idea of how the class will progress, what will be covered, and the activities they'll engage in.
- ❖ Discuss online etiquette and expectations of the students in your first virtual class and periodically revisit the topics.

- ❖ Utilize the Whiteboard or Annotate a shared document and let your students engage as well. When sharing a whiteboard, document, screen, or image, try whiteboarding math problems or have a student use annotation to highlight items such as grammar mistakes in a paper you're sharing.

- ❖ Take time to promote questions, comments, and reactions from your class. Give a minute to allow your students to utilize reactions, write their questions in chat, or be unmuted to ask their questions live.

- ❖ Divide into smaller groups for a discussion on a certain topic. You can use Zoom's Breakout Room feature to either pre-assign or auto-assign students into groups for a short period so they may discuss things together.

- ❖ Have students be the presenter and share projects with the class. This allows your students to show what they're working on while practicing their presentation skills. It also allows students to hear from one another.

Teaching Over Video – Delivery Tips And Tricks

❖ Pre-set your meeting to mute participant's microphones upon entry. This helps to avoid background noise and allow your students to focus on your lesson.

❖ Look at the camera to create eye contact with your students. This helps to create a more personal connection while teaching over video.

❖ Take a second to check chat or your student's video (if on camera) to check-in with your students and get feedback.

❖ Speak as if you're face-to-face with the class while ensuring you're at the appropriate distance from the microphone for the best audio experience.

❖ When delivering a presentation, sharing images, files, or videos, give your students a moment to open or take in what you've shared.

❖ Embrace the pause. Take a moment after the end of your comments and allow for students to engage before continuing.

❖ Teaching with zoom

Tips For Running Large Meeting Sessions

❖ Have a co-presenter to help facilitate the Zoom session with you; especially if you are allowing chat messages and in case you have any unexpected issues.

- ❖ Ensure your session is well planned and it has opportunities for the attendees to actively engage to keep their attention.

- ❖ Add your notes and changes to this checklist, such as 'what went well' and 'what could be improved in the future'.

Great Tools Built Into Zoom For Engagement

- ❖ Attendee Attention Tracking
- ❖ Polling
- ❖ Breakout Rooms
- ❖ Non-verbal Feedback
- ❖ Virtual Backgrounds
- ❖ Sharing a Screen
- ❖ Whiteboard
- ❖ Annotation
- ❖ Transcription of meetings
- ❖ Chat

What Are The Safest Settings For Zoom Meetings?

Zoom was originally intended to be used in business settings, where most folks try their best to act professionally. Kids, not so much. That's why both teachers and students need to know the best settings and features to use to boost learning and minimize disruption. Teachers can prevent Zoombombing, for example, by requiring participants to register for the meeting or use a password, and by disabling screen sharing. Here are a few key settings for keeping the peace in class.

1. **Random Meeting ID:** Though you can use the same meeting ID for every class, Zoom recommends teachers use random meeting IDs (which is an option when they're

creating the invitation). It's less convenient, but it's more secure.

2. **Meeting Password:**These are turned on by default for education users. When a participant manually enters a meeting ID, they are prompted to enter the password.

3. **Mute:** Participants can and should mute themselves when they're not speaking. Teachers can also mute students individually or all at once and can set up the meeting to automatically mute all participants upon entering.

4. **Chat:** The teacher can control whether students can chat publicly and privately during a meeting.

5. **Disable video:** As a participant, you can join the meeting with audio only and then turn on the video once you're ready. Teachers can also disable an individual participant's video.

6. **Nonverbal Feedback:** These optional little icons let students raise their hands, give a thumbs-up or thumbs-down, and even let the teacher know they need a break, all without interrupting the class.

7. **Lock The Meeting:** Remember when your stickler-for-punctuality algebra teacher used to lock the classroom door after the bell rang? Teachers can lock a Zoom meeting so no one else can enter until the teacher personally approves them.

8. **Waiting Rooms:** This is like a lobby or a velvet rope at a club: Participants are held in a virtual room, and the

teacher admits them one by one to make sure no outsiders gain access.

9. **Turn Off File Transfer:** Students can share memes, GIFs, and even quiz answers through the chat -- unless the teacher disables this feature.

What Can Students Do in Zoom?

Besides just voice-chatting, Zoom gives students plenty of tools to interact with each other and the teacher, work together, and even break off into smaller groups just as if they were sitting with each other in a classroom. But if teachers don't need these capabilities for class, or if they're causing problems, they can all be turned off. With a little preparation -- setting some norms and frontloading key digital citizenship skills -- you and your students can enjoy the benefits of Zoom's interactive features. Here's just a sampling of what you can do if these features are enabled:

1. **Share Screen:** This allows the entire class to view one person's computer screen. Students can even annotate a document on another student's computer. Teachers can restrict this so only the teacher's screen can be shared. Teachers can also disable the annotation feature so students can't annotate.

2. **Whiteboard:** This is a brainstorming tool that lets students toss ideas around, such as for a group project.

3. **Breakout Rooms:** The teacher can divide students up into smaller groups, then bring the entire class back together. Teachers can pre-assign the groups before class, assign them manually during the meeting, or have Zoom

randomly break students into groups. (Get more information on breakout rooms here.)

4. **Raise Hand, Clap, Disagree, Speed Up, Slow Down:** These are icons students can use to let the teacher know they have a question or comment, react to something, or ask the teacher to talk faster or slower.

5. **Chat With The Group:** Students can send a message to the entire class.

6. **Private Chat:** Just like passing notes, students can send direct, personal messages to other kids in the class. The teacher can't view private chats between students. The teacher can disable this feature for students.

How Can Teachers Use Zoom?

Teachers are using Zoom in different ways, depending on their skills, their students' needs, and direction from their districts. Here are a few specific ways teachers can use Zoom for distance learning:

1. Record And Share Lessons: Because many students do not have reliable internet at home or are sharing devices with other family members, asynchronous lessons where students can view prerecorded lessons on their schedules make distance learning more equitable. You can use the recording feature in Zoom to create video lessons, then share the videos with students to watch later.

2. Teach Live Lessons: For schools and districts that have solved the technology access issue, synchronous or live lessons are an option. Teachers set up a regular class time on Zoom and guide students through remote learning activities.

3. Flip The Classroom: With the "flipped" classroom model, teachers assign students new material to learn on their own (videos, reading assignments, etc.), then use class time to help clarify the new information and put it to use. Use your live Zoom classes to answer questions about what students learned, and lead them in activities to apply their new knowledge.

4. Office Hours: Some teachers are scheduling regular "office hours," which allow students to drop in and chat informally with teachers and peers.

5. Circle Time, Storytime, Or Show-And-Tell Days: For pre-K and elementary school students, teachers are using Zoom to provide continuity and community. Little ones can't hang with video conferencing for too long, but they do enjoy a chance to see their friends, listen to a story, and show off their toys, pets, baby sisters, and the like.

Useful Teaching Features

1. Text Chat

You can use the chatbox, accessed from the bottom of the screen, to send messages to students during class. You can control how the learners use the chat feature by selecting who they can chat with from the "More" dropdown menu. By default, group chat is enabled. You can choose to limit learners to only chatting with you, the host. Or, to disable chat completely, you should choose the "No one" option. There is not a 1:1 student messaging option, so you don't have to worry about students private messaging each other while you're trying to teach.

2. Screen Sharing

Perhaps Zoom's most useful teaching feature, screen share lets learners see what is on your computer screen. This could include a Powerpoint presentation, a website, a video, or anything else on your computer that would be useful for the class. Zoom also includes a built-in whiteboard as a screen share option, which can be very helpful for many classes. To share your screen, click the green button at the bottom of your Zoom window, then select the option that you wish to share. Remember to check the use computer sound checkbox on the bottom left of the screen share window if you wish to share a video with students, otherwise, the audio will register as background noise on your side and will not be sent into the video classroom.

3. Annotation

Zoom also gives you the option to annotate while screen sharing. This allows you to make your class more interactive since you can draw arrows on Powerpoints, underline complicated words in articles, and do other helpful actions to help students follow along with the material. You'll see the annotation option at the top of the screen while you're screen sharing. Students also have access to the same annotation tools.

If you click on the "More" dropdown menu at the top of the screen, you will have the ability to control the annotation settings. You can:

Enable/Disable Attendee Annotation: This can be useful if the students are using the annotation tools in a distracting manner

Breakout Rooms

Zoom provides a way for you to break students into separate video chat rooms to complete discussion exercises or other group work.

Show/Hide Names Of Annotators: If you have multiple learners annotating on your shared screen, you can hover over the annotation to see which learner created it.

Chapter 5: Creating Your Zoom Virtual Classroom

Zoom offers you the ability to password-protect your virtual classrooms, lock entrance into the classroom after the session has started, and turn off the chat feature. Zoom also provides virtual waiting rooms, so that you can elect not to let unfamiliar users and likely trolls in.

Classroom to classroom collaboration is also possible with a Zoom account, which is especially ideal for younger students who may study different school subjects with different instructors. Perhaps best of all, Zoom allows you to both record and share your video and audio classroom sessions and any other classroom documents with your students. Zoom even provides a transcript of these sessions, allowing students to go over material they didn't understand a second or even third time. Zoom does offer a free video-conferencing plan for K-12 educators that removes the 40-minute time limit on meetings. Note that your institution will need to fill out Zoom's verification form to receive it.

How To Create A Virtual Classroom With Zoom

When creating effective virtual classrooms for the first time, educators will need to focus on the possibilities and benefits video conferencing software provides as opposed to the limitations it places on students and teachers. The good news is that 85% of students say that learning online either replicated or exceeded classroom learning. College-aged students prefer a virtual classroom to a physical one.

After all, in a traditional learning environment, absent students would need to either attempt to decipher classroom notes accessible in Blackboard or borrow notes from another student. But with virtual learning, students can watch the recording of the class they missed and/or read the transcript. This way, they don't fall behind. Plus, these recordings of classes elevate the kind of test prep students have access to. If there's a concept they don't understand, they can simply re-watch you teaching it until they grasp it. It's much easier to build a powerful virtual learning environment when you understand the technical side of things, clearly set student expectations, and look for features that keep both students and teachers engaged.

Virtual Zoom Classrooms

❖ Are an online replacement for physical classrooms on campus.
❖ Provide the option to meet via Zoom with your students at the scheduled class time, in a virtual online room with the same room number as your physical classroom.
❖ Can be accessed from anywhere with an internet connection, including from a computer, laptop, tablet, or smartphone.
❖ Do not require a personal Zoom account or Zoom login.

Features and Security Settings

The following settings have been applied to all Virtual Zoom Classrooms:

❖ Attendees are not hosts, and cannot share their screen or otherwise control the meeting.

- ❖ Everyone joining the meeting has their audio muted by default on entry.

Note: Please ask your students not to share Zoom log-in links, for security reasons.

Instructors Can Upgrade Their Access To 'Host' To Control The Meeting:

- ❖ As the Instructor, you must use the 'Claim Host' option to control the meeting, which includes managing participants and screen-sharing.
- ❖ You will show as a regular participant until you do so.
- ❖ You will find the 'key' for 'claiming host' for each of your courses in the Class Notes Portal.

To 'Claim Host' When Logged Into The Virtual Zoom Classroom:

- ❖ Click "Participants" at the bottom center of the zoom window, within the Participants section click "Claim Host" on the lower right side of the Participants list. Enter the 5-digit key when prompted.
- ❖ To learn more, view the 5-minute how-to claim host video.

Additional Settings That Can Be Controlled By The Meeting Host:

- ❖ Lock the meeting to prevent anyone else from joining.

Note: If a student has technical difficulties and needs to rejoin the meeting, they would also be locked out and prevented from rejoining.

- ❖ Assign a host to another individual, to allow them to share their screen if required.

❖ If using a Zoom Virtual classroom, you may want to consider having some indicator, a small sign within the video frame somehow, to minimize the chance of students being in the wrong room.

Joining The Virtual Zoom Classroom Meeting

❖ Shortly before the scheduled class time, log in to the Class Notes Portal to access the zoom link, meeting ID, password, and host key for your room.
❖ Click the link to connect to the Virtual Zoom Classroom meeting.
❖ Once connected, use the "Claim Host" option to take control of the meeting:
❖ Click "Participants" at the bottom center of the Zoom window.
❖ Within the Participants section click "Claim Host" on the lower right side of the Participants list.
❖ If the option is not showing, click the ... menu to access additional choices.
❖ Enter the 5-digit host key when prompted.
❖ Please do not access a Virtual Zoom Classroom outside of your designated class time. The schedule for use is the same as for the corresponding physical classroom.

How Do You Keep Order In A Zoom Classroom?

When you begin your lesson, ensure that everyone can hear you and that their Zoom screen is working properly. Consider creating a hand signal (a peace sign always works) or a phrase like "Tech Error" to type into chat when someone loses connection or encounters another tech issue.

Make sure you give your students time to open up, download, and view files you've shared with the class. Remember, not everyone has high-speed Internet! Also, pause every so often to ensure that students have time to ask questions before you move onto the next topic.

Talk with your students and develop a code of conduct for your virtual classroom. Students need to understand that your expectations for behavior haven't changed just because the format of your classroom has.

Best Practices For Online Learning

Finally, make the most of distance learning by:

- ❖ Posting lesson plans for the day on your virtual whiteboard
- ❖ Using the attention tracker to monitor students
- ❖ Going on virtual field trips
- ❖ Collaborating with other local and international schools/educators via video
- ❖ Conducting a virtual study hall
- ❖ Pre-recording lessons so you can grade, speak with parents/admins, and plan ahead
- ❖ Locking out late students to maintain a sense of normalcy
- ❖ Having "open office hours" virtually for parents/students
- ❖ Meeting with coworkers virtually
- ❖ Assigning virtual group projects as homework
- ❖ Implementing regular breaks and quick stretch breaks
- ❖ Creating mental health resources for students with guidance counselors

Securing Your Virtual Classroom

Zoom has helped thousands of schools and teachers around the world quickly shift to remote virtual learning, and we want all of them to have the same production environment as their traditional classroom settings. Zoom comes pre-stocked with numerous security features designed to control online classrooms, prevent disruption, and help educators effectively teach remotely. Here are some best practices for securing your virtual classroom using Zoom.

How To Lock Your Classroom

Control Screen Sharing

To give instructors more control over what students are seeing and prevent them from sharing random content, Zoom recently updated the default screen-sharing settings for our education users. Sharing privileges are now set to "Host-Only," so teachers by default are the only ones who can share content in class. However, if students need to share their work with the group, you can allow screen sharing in the host controls. Click the arrow next to Share Screen and then Advanced Sharing Options. Under "Who can share?" choose "Only Host" and close the window. You can also change the default sharing option to All Participants in your Zoom settings.

Enable The Waiting Room

The Waiting Room feature is one of the best ways to protect your Zoom virtual classroom and keep out those who aren't supposed to be there. When enabled, you have two options for who hits the Waiting Room before entering a class:

❖ All Participants will send everyone to the virtual waiting area, where you can admit them individually or all at once.

❖ Guest Participants Only allows known students to skip the Waiting Room and join but sends anyone not signed in/part of your school into the virtual waiting area.

- ❖ The Virtual Waiting Room can be enabled for every class (in your settings) or individual classes at the scheduling level.

Lockdown The Chat

Teachers can restrict the in-class chat so students cannot privately message other students. We'd recommend controlling chat access in your in-meeting toolbar controls (rather than disabling it altogether) so students can still interact with the teacher as needed.

Remove A Participant

If someone who's not meant to be there somehow manages to join your virtual classroom, you can easily remove them from the Participants menu. Hover over their name, and the Remove option (among other options) will appear.

Security Options When Scheduling A Class

The cool thing about Zoom is that you have these and other protection options at your fingertips when scheduling a class and before you ever have to change anything in front of your students. Here are a few of the most applicable:

1. Require Registration: This shows you every email address of everyone who signed up to join your class and can help you evaluate who's attending.

2. Use A Random Meeting ID: It's best practice to generate a random meeting ID for your class, so it can't be shared multiple times. This is the better alternative to using your Meeting ID, which is not advised because it's an ongoing meeting that's always running.

3. Protect The Classroom: Create a passcode and share with your students via school email so only those intended to join can access a virtual classroom.

4. Allow Only Authenticated Users To Join: Checking this box means only members of your school who are signed into their Zoom account can access this particular class.

5. Disable Join Before Host: Students cannot join the class before the teacher joins and will see a pop-up that says, "The meeting is waiting for the host to join."

6. Manage Annotation: Teachers should disable participant annotation in the screen sharing controls to prevent students from annotating on a shared screen and disrupting class.

Additionally, teachers have a couple of in-meeting options to control your virtual classroom:

1. Disable Video: Turn off a student's video to block distracting content or inappropriate gestures while class is in session.

2. Mute Students: Mute/unmute individual students or all of them at once. Mute Upon Entry (in your settings) is also available to keep the clamor at bay when everyone files in.

3. Attendee On-Hold: An alternative to removing a user, you can momentarily disable their audio/video connections. Click on the attendee's video thumbnail and select Start Attendee On-Hold to activate.

An Important Recommendation For Teachers

Teachers: We encourage you to NOT post pictures of your virtual class on social media or elsewhere online. While it's fun to share in the excitement of connecting over Zoom, we are particularly committed to protecting the privacy of K-12 users and discourage publicly posting images of students, especially minors, in a Zoom virtual classroom.

Get Zooming Securely

You can also check out this video on securing your virtual classroom from the Zoom team:

- ❖ Additionally, we've compiled several great resources to help teachers and administrators even the most technology-challenged ones get quickly trained on Zoom and pick up some best practices for educating over Zoom.

How To Set Up A Zoom Quiz

Making The quiz Itself

Within video conferencing apps, such as Zoom, there are often polling and Q&A features available. Most virtual quiz hosts however tend to ask questions themselves and let the participants either mark their answers or send them to the quizmaster over messenger or email.

The first thing you'll want to do before setting up a quiz is to determine the sorts of rounds you'll want - basing this on the demographic of participants. You don't want to have a whole round on sport if everyone in the group hates that subject. Each round usually consists of around 10 questions but as host, you're in control, so it's all about what you want. The quiz can be as short or as long as you want and as easy or as difficult as you like. Once you've decided on the number of questions and the rough categories, you'll want to start formulating the questions.

Two ways make this process particularly easy and will save you time in the long-run.

Firstly, take inspiration (or questions) from other quizzes by having a look around online. Pay particular attention to any that focus on your category and either use a few questions directly - or reverse the question. This is essentially rephrasing the question or changing the parameters slightly. For example, if another quiz asks 'which Kardashian is the oldest?', you could instead ask either of the following:

- ❖ Which sister is the youngest?
- ❖ Which sister was born in 1984?
- ❖ Which sisters were not born in the 1980s?

If you're struggling for inspiration, check out our general knowledge quiz here and feel free to take the questions for your quiz.

The second method of formulating questions is to source the information yourself. You'll need to start by thinking of a topic, theme, or person - for example, Henry VIII. A quick internet search, particularly on Wikipedia, will highlight the main points of interest concerning the topic - in this case, the political achievements, scandal, and personal life of the former monarch.

You then need to choose one aspect to be the focus of the question, so we'll go with his six wives - which is the type of topic popular amongst quizzes and something most people have a basic knowledge of. The information available online reveals the order of the wives, how they died and their relationship to Henry VIII, so it's just a matter of deciding on a more zoned-in aspect. You now have to formulate the question, using what you've read online - for example: "Which of Henry VIII's wives was beheaded first?". The answer, by the way, is Anne Boleyn.

Formulating the quiz is arguably the fun part and it's pretty simple and self-explanatory. Remember though, there are plenty of resources available online to help provide inspiration, questions, or facts if you need them. And it's also worth noting that you don't necessarily have to create a quiz per se. You could prepare some categories for charades, Pictionary, or any other game that doesn't require aboard.

Setting Up A Zoom Quiz

Once you've completed the questions and prepared yourself for the onslaught of contested answers, you'll need to set up the Zoom meeting itself. The host needs to sign up for an account, which is free, and this gives them the ability to organize a video chat meeting - amongst other features, that we won't go into. As reported by the Telegraph, setting up the Zoom meeting itself varies slightly depending on the device being used by the host - but the process is generally as follows. Once logged in, you need to click 'host a meeting' on the web, or 'new meeting' on the desktop or mobile apps. You'll then want to select 'call using internet audio' and after that point, it's perhaps a good idea to go to the Security features and switch on 'Enable Waiting Room' which allows you to screen who enters the video call.

So you're now on the call, though you're alone, so it's time to add participants. To do this, select 'Manage Participants' and 'Invite' - which will give you the option to invite via email or to Zoom contacts. Additionally, you can copy the URL and share it on other social media apps or via text message. Once an invitee clicks the link, they'll be sent to the Waiting Room so be sure to check to Manage Participants every so often to move them into the call itself - and once everyone's in, you can 'lock meeting' to prevent additional participants. It's important to note that Zoom's free service limits group calls of three people or more to 40 minutes - so the host will either have to temporarily end the chat at that point or upgrade for £11.99 a month. Additionally, some participants may be concerned about using Zoom following claims which surfaced online recently.

How To Run The Best Zoom Quiz: Tips For quizzing Success

Zoom has evolved into the tool of choice for keeping people connected, but one surprising trend that's emerged is quizzes. Quizzes work so well on Zoom because they're social, while not needing people to shout across the top of each other all the time.

Essentially, it's a way of getting a group of people together, engaged in an activity, without having to take turns in talking. From a business tool to quizzing cool, here are some tips on how to run the ultimate quiz from home.

Get Yourself Prepared

Every quiz master needs to start with a quiz and every quiz needs structure - and the most important parts of running a quiz happen offline, or rather, in the planning.

Make A Presentation

First of all, you need your questions. As you're going to be running this over Zoom, instead of reading all your questions and struggling with people not being able to hear, make a presentation. That can be in PowerPoint, Keynote, Slides, or anything else - and we think Slides works well, with the advantage of being free. The key thing here is to make a presentation that makes your quiz pop - because everyone else is going to see this. As always practice, practice, practice, get your transitions or effects organized, so you know what you're doing.

The advantage of using a presentation is that you can embed everything in that presentation a picture round, quotes to complete, music round, whatever you like. Put it into "present" and/or full-screen mode, so those on the presentation can't see the rest of your desktop.

Top Tip: put each question on a different slide, so you can click through easily, or back if you need to.

Prepare Your Computer And Network

It's worth shutting down everything else you don't need - to quit and exit Skype, Word, Photoshop - anything that could be running in the background that you don't need, as Zoom is a demanding app. As you'll be sharing your screen, all you want open is the things you need to share - and the fewer programs you have open, the less Zoom will offer you when it comes to sharing.

Prepare Your Answers

A great way to make your quiz easier is to use an answer sheet. Sure, people can just write answers on a bit of paper, but preparing an answer sheet means people know where they are, how many questions to expect and you can make the structure of your quiz a little more complicated - for example with two-part answers, picture rounds and so on. Once you've built your quiz, put together your answer sheet and send it through with the invitation or meeting details and people can just print it off at home.

Consider What Everyone Is Seeing And Hearing

Remember that as the host, people are likely to be looking at, and listening to you more than any other participant, so think about what you have in the background, and what noise there is around you. Silence your phone to avoid those annoying bings and bongs, and don't sit next to your fridge or washing machine on the spin cycle. Also don't sit with your back to a window or patio doors, because you'll be silhouetted. A nice plain background is simple; a studious-looking bookcase is very much on-trend right now, or you can pick a Zoom background.

Use The Power Of Zoom

Zoom, as a tool for businesses first and foremost, has a collection of features that are useful when presenting your quiz - and the main one here is the ability to share your screen, so you can show off that presentation and people can get involved with professional experience.

Setting Up A Zoom Meeting

Zoom meetings can be scheduled, or you can just go in and start a meeting and get others to join. For something organized like a quiz, it's great to schedule it for the time you want it to take place, sharing the meeting ID and password via whatever means you want. If scheduling a meeting, those ID and passwords are on the scheduling page for you.

If you've started a new meeting, you can find the details by clicking the "i" in the top left corner and sharing - but be organized, and schedule instead. If you are scheduling, you can setup a lot of the parameters of the meeting in advance, including allowing people in before you (the host) is there. That's great for social events.

Dealing With That 40-Minute Time Limit

Zoom has a 40-minute time limit on meetings unless you pay for the Pro level ($14.99/£11.99/$13.99 a month). If you're doing a lot of Zooming it be worth paying for a few months until you're released back into the real world - you can cancel at any time. But Zoom has also relaxed the rules a little around this 40-minute restriction. You might be offered the chance to avoid the time limit if you schedule your next Zoom meeting, so that's worth considering. If not, and if you don't want to pay, be prepared to end and restart at an opportune moment. That also allows toilet breaks and drink refreshes - and you can always share multiple meeting IDs in advance.

Share Your Presentation And Off You Go

Once you're up and running with your meeting, you need to share your presentation. This is easy and something that Zoom is good at, which is why it's perfect for quizzes. Just hit the big Share Screen button in the Zoom toolbar and select what it is you want to share - your presentation. You'll want that application to be in the present model, so it fills the screen and you're not showing off your desktop wallpaper, shortcuts, and all the rest of it. When you go into the screen sharing option you'll find some advanced settings, including the option to limit screen sharing to just you, the host. You'll want to check this option, so no one else can disrupt things and start presenting something else from their end.

Turn Off Annotations

Zoom allows annotations by default, allowing participants to add annotations to screens that are shared. That means anyone in your quiz can draw on your presentation - but you can turn this off. Unfortunately, these are in the advanced options of your Zoom account accessed via Zoom's web portal. If you open up the preferences for the Zoom app you can get to these by heading into the profile, then "view advanced features". This opens the web page for your account and down that page, you'll find "annotation" with the option to switch off access for participants.

Use The Power of Mute

Once your quiz is underway, you'll need to keep control of the rabble. People will probably mute themselves if they want to discuss it as a team, but you'll also have the power as the host to mute the entire quiz. You'll find this option in participants in the toolbar - where you can mute and unmute everyone. There's the option for people to unmute themselves - which you can also turn off if you want to.

Importantly, muting will mean that people can hear what you're saying. If you have to explain the rules of a round or give any pointers, definitely mute the rabble - and you'll want to mute all for the music round too if you have one. But don't leave things muted all the time, as this will then dampen the social feeling to the quiz - people will still want to talk, laugh, and interact. As you're using a presentation people can read the questions themselves so a little noise isn't going to spoil things.

Tips For Writing The Best Quiz Questions

- ❖ Question: Who writes the best personality quizzes?
- ❖ Answer: You, after reading this article.

When you are creating a personality quiz, one of the most important and most challenging elements are the questions. You want to make a quiz that's fun to take, and following the tips below will mean your quiz is sure to be a hit.

1. Aim For 7 questions

With 7 questions, your quiz is long enough to cover the subject but quick enough to be easily completed. To make sure all 7 questions are the best they can be, start by brainstorming 14 questions and then eliminate any that aren't fun, are too difficult, or don't correlate well with the outcomes.

2. Keep It Short And Simple

Questions shouldn't require too much thought to answer, so the question itself should be just a simple sentence. As for answers, one word is best, but 2-4 word phrases are OK in moderation.

3. Don't Make Your Questions Too Obvious

If you are writing a What Kind of Car Should You Drive? quiz, don't make one of the questions "What kind of car do you want?" While that may be an extreme example, but you should make sure that none of your questions or answers point too obvious to a particular outcome. Also, keep in mind that your questions don't necessarily need to be related to the topic of the quiz. As long as the question has a purpose and helps lead to an outcome, it can be about anything.

4. Pay Attention To The Order Of Your questions

To capture people's attention, start your quiz with your second-most exciting question, and then finish it off with the most exciting to go out with a bang. Keep the most difficult questions that might require more thought in the middle, so that by the time people get to them they are already committed.

5. Have A Consistent Number Of Answers

Each question you write should have the same number of answers unless you have a specific reason for changing that number (i.e. a Yes or No answer). A good number of answers to aim for is 4-6. You should also make an effort to vary the punch line, by sometimes putting the funniest answer at the end and sometimes leading with it.

6. Make Sure There's An Answer For Everyone

When you are writing the answers, make them all uniquely different, and cover the full spectrum so everyone can select an answer that works for them. One useful strategy is to think of your answers in terms of high, medium, low, and no interest. One answer is for someone extremely interested in the topic, one is for someone with an average interest, one is for someone mildly interested, and one is for someone with no interest in the topic at all.

7. Be Careful With Pop Culture References

When you are considering using a pop culture reference in your quiz (i.e. "Who is your favorite sitcom character?"), first consider your target audience will they get these references? Make sure all of the people or characters you include are widely recognizable since people might give up on your quiz if they don't know any of them and aren't able to make an informed decision for their response.

The most important thing to remember when creating a quiz is to leave time for testing. Send your completed quiz around to your friends, coworkers, and family members, and make sure they enjoy the process of taking it and are happy with their outcomes before you make it public.

Classroom Problem

Are Your Students Getting It?

Students seldom tell you what they don't know!. They are too embarrassed to raise their hand when they don't get a concept. Instructors often mistake silence for student understanding and press on before students are ready...or spend too much time on material students got the first time.

Zoom Solution: Zoom now allows for real-time polling on the fly, which can be used as a Classroom Assessment Technique (CAT) to assess the general knowledge of the class about a specific topic. At any point in the lecture, the instructor can pose a question to check for student understanding. Problems can be presented with multiple choice answers. or just a simple scale of confidence:

- ❖ "Can solve."
- ❖ "Might be able to."
- ❖ "Clueless."

Students answer anonymously, and the instructor can immediately see where the class stands...and can probe deeper if needed, or press on...if they get the green light.

How Can I Use A Zoom Poll To Assess Comprehension?

Polls can be a great tool for quick, real-time formative assessment in your virtual class sessions or meetings. Using polls can help you gauge where your students are in terms of their comprehension of the material you're presenting (as well as whether or not they're actively paying attention)!. Zoom has a polling feature that allows you to ask a question with multiple choice answers and view and save meeting participants' responses.

The polling feature for meetings allows you to create a single choice or multiple choice polling questions for your meetings. You will be able to launch the poll during your meeting and gather the responses from your attendees. You also can download a report on polling after the meeting. Polls can also be conducted anonymously if you do not wish to collect participant information with the poll results.

This Article Covers:

- ❖ Enabling polling
- ❖ Account
- ❖ Group
- ❖ User
- ❖ Creating a Poll
- ❖ Launching a Poll

Downloading A Report Of Poll Results

Prerequisites

Host user type must be Licensed

- ❖ Windows Desktop Client Version 3.5.63382.0829 or higher
- ❖ Mac Desktop Client Version 3.5.63439.0829 or higher
- ❖ Linux Desktop Client version 2.0.70790.1031 or higher

The meeting must be either a scheduled meeting or an instant meeting using your Meeting ID

Participants on the iOS or Android mobile app can use polling, but hosts need to be using the desktop client to manage to poll.

Note: Only the original meeting host can edit or add polls during a meeting. If the host or co-host role is transferred to another user, that user will only be able to launch polls already created.

Enabling Polling

Account

To enable the polling feature for all members of your organization:

- ❖ Sign in to the Zoom web portal as an administrator with the privilege to edit account settings.
- ❖ In the navigation menu, click Account Management then Account Settings.
- ❖ Navigate to the Polling option on the Meeting tab and verify that the setting is enabled.
- ❖ If the setting is disabled, click the toggle to enable it. If a verification dialog displays, choose Turn On to verify the change.
- ❖ (Optional) If you want to make this setting mandatory for all users in your account, click the lock icon, and then click Lock to confirm the setting.

Group

To enable the Polling feature for all members of a specific group:

- ❖ Sign in to the Zoom web portal as an administrator with the privilege to edit user groups.
- ❖ In the navigation menu, click User Management then Group Management.
- ❖ Click the name of the group, then click the Settings tab.
- ❖ Navigate to the Polling option on the Meeting tab and verify that the setting is enabled.
- ❖ If the setting is disabled, click the toggle to enable it. If a verification dialog displays, choose Turn On to verify the change.

Note: If the option is grayed out, it has been locked at the Account level, and needs to be changed at that level.

- ❖ (Optional) If you want to make this setting mandatory for all users in this group, click the lock icon, and then click Lock to confirm the setting.

User

To enable Polling for your use:

- ❖ Sign in to the Zoom web portal.
- ❖ In the navigation menu, click Account Management then Account Settings (if you are an account administrator) or Settings (if you are an account member).
- ❖ Navigate to the Polling option on the Meeting tab and verify that the setting is enabled.
- ❖ If the setting is disabled, click the toggle to enable it. If a verification dialog displays, choose Turn On to verify the change.

Note: If the option is grayed out, it has been locked at either the Group or Account level, and you will need to contact your Zoom administrator.

Creating A Poll

- ❖ Go to the Meetings page and click on your scheduled meeting. If you do not have a scheduled meeting, schedule a meeting now.
- ❖ From the meeting management page, scroll to the bottom to find the Poll option. Click Add to begin creating the poll.
- ❖ Enter a title and your first question.
- ❖ (Optional) Check the box to make the poll anonymous, which will keep the participant's polling information anonymous in the meeting and the reports.
- ❖ Select whether you want the question to be a single choice(participants can only choose one answer) or multiple-choice questions (participants can choose multiple answers).
- ❖ Type in the answers to your question and click Save at the bottom.

- ❖ If you would like to add a new question, click Add a Question to create a new question for that particular poll.
- ❖ You can add more polls by repeating Step 2.
- ❖ You can also create a poll by clicking Polling during the meeting. This will open up your default web browser where you can add additional polls or questions.

Note: You can only create a max of 25 polls for a single meeting.

Launching A Poll

- ❖ Start the scheduled Zoom meeting that has polling enabled.
- ❖ Click Polls in the meeting controls.
- ❖ Select the poll you would like to launch.
- ❖ Click Launch Poll.
- ❖ The participants in the meeting will now be prompted to answer the polling questions. The host will be able to see the results live.
- ❖ Once you would like to stop the poll, click End Poll.
- ❖ If you would like to share the results with the participants in the meeting, click Share Results.
- ❖ Participants will then see the results of the polling questions.

Downloading A Report Of Poll Results

You can download a report on the poll results after the meeting. When viewing a report of the poll results, take note of these things:

- ❖ If registration was turned on and the poll was not anonymous, it will list the participants' names and email addresses.
- ❖ If registration was not on, the polling report will show the profile names of authenticated users in the same account.

- If the poll was anonymous, it will show "anonymous" for the participants' names and email addresses.

How Do I Record Students' Grades Or Assignments Or Quizzes?

Import Grades To Classroom

If you attach a quiz to an assignment, you can import grades from Forms to Classroom's Student Work page. However, if you attach a form as a link in the Classroom, you can't import student grades. For details, go to Create a quiz assignment. When you import grades, all grades are imported. You can't select some grades to import. If you don't want to import all grades, you can enter them manually on the Classroom Student Work page. For details, go to Import grades.

To Import Grades:

- The quiz must be the only attachment to the assignment.
- Students are limited to 1 response.
- Students must be in the same domain as you.
- Student email addresses must be collected.
- If you change any of these settings after you save or post the assignment, grade importing might be turned off and you might not be able to import grades.

Import Quiz Grades Before Grading Other Work

Importing quiz grades will override any current grades for the assignment. Import the quiz grades first. Then, grade any other work on the assignment.

Edit An Assignment After You Import Grades

If you edit an assignment after you turn on grade importing and post an assignment, grade importing might get turned off. For example, if you add another attachment or change a setting that's needed to import grades, grade importing is turned off.

Change Grades After Importing

The grades in Forms and Classroom are separate. If you change the grades in Forms after you import them to the Classroom, click Import grades to bring the new grades into the Classroom, and overwrite the previous grades you imported.

See All Answers At A Glance

- ❖ Go to classroom.google.com.
- ❖ Click the class and than classwork.
- ❖ On the quiz assignment, click the quiz attachment.
- ❖ Click Edit "and then respond.

Return Grades To Students

- ❖ Go to classroom.google.com.
- ❖ Click the class and than classwork.
- ❖ Click the quiz assignment.
- ❖ On the left, select the students you want to return grades to.
- ❖ Click Return and thenReturn to confirm.
- ❖ Students get their grades immediately.
- ❖ To check their grades, on the Classwork page, students can click the quiz attachment and then View score.

Note: You can let students see their grade immediately after they submit their answers

Create A Quiz Assignment

When you create a quiz assignment, Classroom creates a blank quiz using Google Forms and attaches the form to the assignment. You can then edit the quiz and add questions. You can also lock a quiz on Chromebooks and import grades.

Before You Begin

When you create a quiz assignment, you have many of the same options as to when you create an assignment or a question. You can:

- ❖ Post the quiz to individual students or one or more classes
- ❖ Add a due date and time
- ❖ Add attachments
- ❖ Schedule it to post later
- ❖ Reuse a quiz

You also have additional Google Forms features. You can add point values, give feedback, and release the student's grade after they submit their answers.

Create And Edit Quizzes

- ❖ Go to classroom.google.com.
- ❖ Click the class and than classwork.
- ❖ At the top, click Create and then quiz assignment.
- ❖ Create a Quiz assignment
- ❖ Enter the title and any instructions.
- ❖ (Optional) To prevent students from opening other pages during the quiz, next to Locked mode on Chromebooks, click Turn on ".
- ❖ (Optional) To import grades, next to Grade importing, click Turn on ".

Note: If you change the name of the quiz in Drive, the name is updated in the Classroom.

Import Grades

You can import the grades into the Classroom when your students are done taking the quiz. Importing grades overwrites manually assigned grades.

If You Import Grades

- ❖ The form is limited to one response per user.
- ❖ The user's email address is collected automatically.
- ❖ Only users in your domain can respond to the form.

Import Grades

- ❖ Go to classroom.google.com.
- ❖ Click a class and than classwork.
- ❖ Click the quiz assignment and then view the Assignment.
- ❖ On the Student Work page, click Import Grades.

Note: If you don't see Import grades, your form wasn't set up as a quiz or you didn't turn on Grade importing when you created the assignment.

- ❖ Click Import.
- ❖ The classroom enters grades for each student. If you didn't assign points, the assignment is labeled ungraded.

See Student Answers

- ❖ Go to classroom.google.com.
- ❖ Click the class and than classwork.
- ❖ On the quiz assignment, click the quiz attachment.
- ❖ Click Edit and then Responses.

Chapter 6: The Most Common Zoom Problems and How to Fix Them

Telecommuting is on the rise these days, with more companies turning to videoconference to keep their employees in the loop. But nothing is more embarrassing than leading a meeting and having some glitches pop up. Some of us use Zoom for personal calls, too, but no matter the purpose, we don't like problems popping up either. We've collected the most common issues Zoom users face and give you step-by-step ways to fix them.

Webcam Or Audio Not Working

Nothing is more frustrating than having your webcam or audio not work on a Zoom call. If your web camera is not showing up or is selected and is not working on Zoom, then you might want to try some of these basic tips first. When you join a call, Zoom will prompt you with an option to Join with Video before entering the meeting. Always click this button, or else you will enter the call without your camera feed.

If your web camera isn't showing up, the first thing to do is check to make sure all other programs that use the webcam are closed. Zoom won't be able to use the camera if you've already given access to it in a different application. If your webcam or audio still isn't working, you can test your audio and video in Zoom by clicking this link. Once open, you can join the call as usual on the Zoom app, and follow the instructions on the screen.

If you've joined on the web (or to just double-check your webcam in the main Zoom app,) you can also select your webcam by clicking Start Video (it might say Stop Video if you're in a call.) If the screen is blank, you can then click the arrow next to the video camera icon and choose the Same as a system or a more specifically named webcam from the list.

Sometimes, though, the problem might not be Zoom at all. If you're on a Windows 10 or macOS device, the webcam might be blocked. You can correct this by checking your app permissions to make sure the Zoom app or your web browser can use your webcam. On the web specifically, you also can check this setting by restarting your call and making sure you pressed Allow when prompted about the camera and microphone access.

On Windows, you can check to see if your webcam is blocked by searching for Webcam in the Start Menu and selecting Choose which apps can use a camera from the menu. Scroll down and you'll see the list of applications that are allowed to use your webcam. Make sure the box for your web browser or Zoom is ticked. In the same way, you also can search for Microphone and choose Microphone privacy settings to do the same.

On macOS, you'll need to click Security and Privacy in the System Settings, click the lock, and enter your password to make changes. You can then click Camera from the sidebar, and make sure your web browser and Zoom are checked. You'll also want to make sure the box for the microphone is checked, too.

Echoes During A Call

Another common problem with Zoom is an audio echo during a meeting. If you hear audio echo or feedback during your meeting, there are three possible reasons why.

First, someone could have both computer and telephone audio active at the same time. In this case, you'll want to ask them to manually leave one in favor of the other. They'll have to either hang up on the telephone call or leave audio during the conference by clicking the up arrow next to the microphone icon and choosing Leave Computer Audio.

Another cause could be that people with computers or telephone speakers might be too close to each other. Lastly, multiple computers with active audio could be in the same conference room.

To resolve either of these other situations, you'll have to ask the two people that are too close to each other to move apart. Or ask one of them to leave the audio conference or mute audio on their device.

Problems With Zoom Lagging Or Freezing During Meetings

Lagging and freezing usually indicate a problem with your internet connection. If on a mobile device, try to move to an area with more stable internet to see if this helps. You should also aim for the right internet speeds for a successful video chat. In a team setting when you are talking with multiple people, you will want to aim for around a 1Mbps download speed and 800kbps upload speed. You can always check your current speeds with a quick internet speed test.

You may be able to improve video quality by changing your Zoom settings, as well. For example, disabling HD options or the "Touch Up My Appearance" setting will decrease the amount of bandwidth your video connection requires (and the overhead on your system's hardware), and can help fix problems with lag.

Problems Sharing A Screen

If you're planning to share your screen during a call, you might need to check a couple of settings first. Make sure that you have a solid internet connection, and that you're connected to the call. Sharing your screen takes up a lot of bandwidth. It's also a good idea to try a Screen Share meeting first in Zoom. You can do this by selecting Start with no video at the Home tab when starting or joining a meeting. Your meeting will then start with only audioconferencing, freeing up some bandwidth. Your video will not be automatically turned on. Alternatively, if you're already on a call and need to share your screen, try turning off your video by clicking the Stop Video button and then choosing the green Share screen button.

Problems With A Remote Control While Screen Sharing

When screen sharing, the person watching your screen can request remote control to help you troubleshoot or explain a process more clearly under Options is a tool to Request remote control at any time while sharing the screen. If you want to enable remote control but it's not working properly, there are several possible issues to consider:

1. The Sharer Is Not Agreeing To The Request: A notification will pop up on their screen and they will have to choose Allow to share screens.

2. The Sharer Is Interrupting The Process: Technically, the person sharing their screen can stop the remote control at any time by clicking their mouse. In practice, sometimes people are always doing something that ends the remote control session before you can do anything. Always remind people to leave their computers alone while you're assuming remote control.

3. You Could Be On The Wrong Device: iPad and Android devices, for example, currently don't allow requesting or giving remote control.

Problems Receiving Email Messages From Zoom

Another common problem is not being able to receive email messages from Zoom. This can include notifications and activation emails. These usually take 30 minutes to arrive and could take longer, but if it doesn't arrive, you need to make sure that your email is configured properly.

Problems With Zoom Crashing

If Zoom is crashing and closing itself entirely, your first move should be to check Zoom Service Status and Downdetector to see if there is a regional Zoom problem in your area. Sometimes issues with servers or Zoom doing maintenance to the platform, which means the service will be down for a while and you will have to wait for it to come back up again. If it doesn't look regional, we suggest trying the web version of Zoom instead of the app: As long as your internet connection is sufficient, the web version tends to be a bit more reliable if the app is experiencing problems.

Finally, take a look at your peripheral settings. Sometimes Zoom can get very confused about audio versus video settings. If it's trying to use your webcam connection as an audio output, for example, it will often start crashing as a result. Make sure video connections are routed to your webcam and, if necessary, that audio is routed to connected speakers.

Problems With Getting Zoom-Bombed

Zoom bombing is the growing fad of joining a private meeting and disrupting it with anything from blaring music to porn and even courtrooms aren't immune. If you have been Zoom-bombed in the past, there is one solution that is incredibly effective at preventing it from happening again: Requiring a passcode.

The host creating the meeting and sending out invitations can require that participants enter a passcode to join the meeting, which means strangers have a hard time finding ways to drop in. In fact, as of May 2020 updates, requiring a password is set as the default, so all you may need to do is update Zoom and start using this feature.

And if you are worried about hacking in more elaborate ways, there is good news: In June 2020, Zoom announced that it would be bringing end-to-end encryption to all meetings (not just paid versions) to help protect content and prevent more advanced versions of Zoom-bombing even if you are using a free account.

Chapter 7: Zoom Guides to Students and Parents

What Is Zoom?

Zoom is a popular video conferencing platform that is now more commonly used in schools. It's very similar to other video conferencing apps like FaceTime, Skype, or Google Hangouts, except Zoom has cool features that allow for big conferencing groups, virtual whiteboards, and other collaborative resources.

A Student Guide To Zoom

What Can Zoom Be Used For?

Zoom can be used to do many things outside of a regular classroom. Try using Zoom to...

- ❖ Meet with group members for projects and assignments
- ❖ Work on homework with classmates
- ❖ Record a presentation
- ❖ Schedule online tutoring
- ❖ Host a meeting for a club or organization

What Devices Can I Use Zoom On?

- ❖ Laptop/computer (PC/Mac) -- recommended
- ❖ Tablet (Apple iOS, Android)
- ❖ Smartphone (Apple iOS, Android)

Preparing For A Zoom Meeting

How To Schedule A Meeting

Option 1: Scheduling through the desktop app

❖ Open the Zoom desktop app.
❖ Click on the Home button at the top left.
❖ Press the Schedule button.
❖ Enter in Topic, Date, and other related details and press Schedule. It is recommended that you make

Registration required when scheduling a meeting, as that allows you to generate a registration report after the meeting is over.

Days Before

❖ Remember to download and install the Zoom launcher (PC/Mac) or the app (iOS/Android) in advance, as it can take several minutes to complete.
❖ Review Zoom instructions here or via the external Zoom link found in your Moodle or Canvas course.
❖ Join a Zoom Test Meeting (found by clicking here) to confirm your computer or device's capabilities.
❖ In your test meeting, practice using the Zoom features listed below under "Views to Choose From" and "The Zoom Menu."
❖ Contact HSU's IT Help Desk to resolve any technical issues if your test meeting fails.
❖ If you have a disability and need an accommodation such as captioning, contact HSU's Disability Resource.

15 Minutes Before

Find a quiet space with strong WiFi that is free of distractions. You can test your internet connection speed by visiting Zoom's suggested third party bandwidth tester, Speedtest.

Open Zoom via the downloaded program, app, or through the Zoom module link in Moodle or Canvas.

Test your headphones, microphone, and camera to make sure the class can hear and see you (and vice versa).

To test your microphone, click "Test Computer Mic & Speakers" in the pop-up window that appears when first opening a test meeting or beginning your scheduled meeting. More information on audio testing can be found here.

To test your camera, just look at the Zoom window to see that you are visible, non-pixellated, and can move and speak without noticeable delays. Click here for more video testing tips.

You may need to give Zoom permission to access your camera and microphone beforehand. Typically, the request for permission will appear in a pop-up window the first time you open a Zoom Meeting and will carry over to future meetings. If you declined permissions in the past, you will need to go into your PC or Mac's settings to allow Zoom to access your camera and microphone. You can contact the Help Desk to assist you in this process, or find information on the internet for your specific device.

Close any windows or programs open on your device that are unrelated to your meeting. This focuses your device's power to provide the best Zoom meeting experience possible and prevents potential embarrassing moments if you happen to share your screen. Do you want your professor to know how many cat videos you watch?

During The Zoom Meeting

❖ Click Start Video to begin broadcasting from your webcam.

- ❖ Click the Chat bubble to ask questions via text, share links to websites, and keep up with the class's back-channel discussion. You can chat with everyone in the meeting, just the professor, or a specific person.
- ❖ Find out who else is in the meeting by clicking Participants. This is also where you can "raise your hand" to ask a question, answer a question, or start an intense philosophical debate. What you do with this power is up to you.
- ❖ Be prepared to share your screen with the class. They can see the tabs you have open. (Italicized for emphasis, fam.)
- ❖ At the end of the class, click Leave Meeting.

Best Practices While In A Class/Meeting

- ❖ Sign in to the Zoom desktop client and stay signed in.
- ❖ Check your internet speed. If you're on free wifi you may need to keep your camera off to improve quality.
- ❖ Turn your camera on and have your camera at eye level.
- ❖ Stay muted unless you're talking to reduce background noise.
- ❖ Make sure you sit in a well lit and quiet place.
- ❖ Be mindful of what's going on behind you. Think about having a solid wall behind you or turning on the virtual background

A Parent's Guide To Zoom

Zoom has many helpful tools that make it pretty perfect for kids to use with their teachers. These are the features you can expect your kid's teacher to use while teaching them over Zoom.

How Do Teachers Use Zoom?

1. Screen Sharing: Your kid's teacher will likely share their screen to present lessons and demonstrate principles. It's the same idea as your teacher using an overhead in class.

2. Whiteboard: Your kid's teacher may use this tool for kids to brainstorm ideas and participate in lessons.

3. Breakout rooms: Your kid's teacher can divide kids into groups, have them work on something, and then bring the class back together afterward.

4. Special Icons: There are Raise Hand, Clap, Disagree, Speed Up, and Slow Down icons that your kid can use to let the teacher know if they have a comment or are going too fast. Though I'd be careful about letting my kid tell the teacher to "speed up."

5. Group Chat Features: Everyone in the Zoom session can send and receive messages to each other. It's like passing notes, but not as fun or challenging. Your kid's teacher can productively use this feature to have partners exchange ideas and work together.

Make Sure Your Kid Understands The Mute Button

Everyone who isn't actively speaking on Zoom should mute their microphone. Trust us on this one, non-muted mics can turn Zoom into a circus. A recent sketch on Saturday Night Live perfectly captures the point we're trying to make. Muting your microphone on Zoom is easy. Just click the microphone icon on the bottom right once your kid starts a Zoom call. Make sure it has the red slash through it unless they are participating.

How Do I Keep My Child Engaged During Zoom?

Believe it or not, some kids have a hard time focusing on schoolwork while they're on the computer. Hopefully, your kid's teacher does a good job engaging with students via Zoom, but it might be wise to stay in the room for a couple of teaching sessions to make sure your kid isn't surfing the web or playing Fortnite or something.

How to download the Zoom app on your mobile device

- ❖ Open your app store
- ❖ Search for Zoom
- ❖ Hit download

How Do I Make A Zoom Account For My Kid?

Setting up a Zoom account is super simple. Sign up for a free Zoom account here. All your kids will need is an email address to set up their Zoom account.

How Do I Protect My Child On Zoom?

Zoom has had its issues with security over the past few months, but Zoom has been actively working on upgrading its security. Still, you should take every precaution to make sure your kid doesn't get Zoombombed or exposed to anything you don't want them seeing over Zoom.

Make Sure You Have A Reliable Internet Connection

It's hard enough to learn outside of the classroom (also, sometimes in the classroom), but a glitchy Zoom stream will make learning pretty much impossible. You'll want dedicated internet speeds of at least 225 kbps to smoothly run a large group Zoom meeting. If your kid's Zoom stream consistently glitches out, it might be time to upgrade your internet connection. Our internet expert, Catherine, recommends Xfinity internet as the best internet option available right now. If you're not sure what internet providers are available in your area, you can enter your zipcode below to see all of your internet options.

Zoom Basics To Help Get You Started

1. Camera Shy? No Problem: If you've ever been tasked with trying to get a smiling photo of your preteen, you know that some kids just do not want to be in front of the camera. This poses a problem when your child is required to show up virtually for Zoom class meetings. Rather than starting the day off with an argument, there is a simple trick to alleviate this problem. Within the Video tab, simply check "always turn off video when joining a meeting," and your child can rest assured that they will not be seen. This feature is also helpful for parents worried about webcam privacy.

2. Fix That Cluttered Screen: In Gallery View (more on that below) your child has the option to see all Zoom classroom meeting participants. In Zoom, for some kids, the blank spaces on the screen can be overwhelming. A helpful trick you likely never knew is that you do have the capability to remove those blank spaces. In Video settings simply click "hide non-video participants."

3. You're In Control: Teachers may choose to use the screen share feature to show pertinent slides or images to the Zoom conference. For some students, not being able to see the teacher's face as they're speaking can significantly impact comprehension. Within Zoom, your child can easily click on Options to engage Side-by-Side Mode. This will allow your child to toggle between the slide and the teacher as needed. The participant gallery becomes a pop-up that can easily be moved around the screen as needed by your child.

A Note About Safety: Zoom has been a learning curve for many, including parents and kids. There's also the added concern of online safety. With the recent news of Zoom-bombers hacking into the site and disrupting meetings, parents have had to take additional safety precautions. Some ways to do this include using the "waiting room" feature to ensure only approved participants can enter the meeting room, disabling screen-sharing by participants other than the host, and locking the meeting to outsiders.

4. Mute When Necessary: Zoom etiquette is often a difficult concept for kids navigating the give and takes of teleconferencing. Your child's teacher will have the option to Mute All of the class participants when setting up the Zoom classroom. If you find that the teacher has left the mute button open for your child to control, rather than having to search for it on the screen, simply have your child tap the spacebar to either mute or unmute themselves.

5. A Virtual Portrait Gallery: To allow your child to see everyone on the Zoom call, the Gallery View option is a good tip to use if the screen bouncing back and forth between speakers is distracting. In the upper-right corner of the classroom, simply turn on Gallery View.

6. Got A Blank Space?: When a classmate chooses not to participate in the video, their screen will still show up in your View Gallery feature. If your child finds the cluttered screen with blank spaces distracting, you can easily hide classmates that choose not to include their video. This can be done in Settings under the Meetings tab.

7. Sync It Up: Older children who may have their cell phones may consider logging in to Zoom classes via smartphone. One helpful Zoom trick is to sync your child's classroom schedule and assignment due dates to their smartphone calendar application.

8. Simple Is Best: If your young child smiles wide at the sight of their teacher's face on their tablet during virtual circle time, you may be tempted to cast the Zoom class to the large family television. Sometimes, however, simple is best with younger children.

9. Building Life Skills: The biggest tip to remember when it comes to virtual learning is that you and your children are learning technology tricks you likely never knew before. The virtual learning experience has no doubt expanded our skillset as parents, teachers, and students.

Chapter 8: Tip and Tricks

10 Tips And Tricks For Zoom

The best video conferencing apps can do more than merely enable a virtual face-to-face meeting. They let you show what's on your screen to everyone else on the call, seamlessly pass control of the meeting to another person, and record the call as a video. Web conferencing service Zoom offers these features and more, some of the hidden options in advanced menus. The tricks and tips below will show you how to use the app better to work, learn, and communicate with others virtually.

1. Automatically Schedule Meetings And Let People Know About Them

If you run a lot of meetings for example, with clients but don't have an assistant, you might want to connect your scheduling app, Zoom, and your calendar. Whenever someone books an appointment in a scheduling app, for example, Zapier can automatically create a new Zoom meeting and add it to whatever app you use for your calendar. Here are some pre-built Zaps to power this workflow, but you can create a Zap with whatever apps you use.

2. Create Recurring Meetings With Saved Settings And One URL

For weekly meetings, monthly check-ins, and other regularly-scheduled calls, Zoom lets you create a recurring meeting. There are two benefits to using this setting. First, it lets you lock in all the call settings you want once and have them be in place every time you meet. Second, recurring calls use the same join URL each time, so you never have to send a fresh one to attendees.

Additionally, if you meet with the same group regularly but not on a regular schedule, you can choose an option called No Fixed Time, which lets you use the same settings and meeting ID over and over with the same group, no matter when you get together. This option is popular with educational groups who use Zoom as their virtual classroom.

3. See Who Attended

Say you're using Zoom to hold a mandatory event, like a university lecture or a safety training session. You probably want to know who attends. You can get that information from a report once the meeting is finished. The attendee list for all meetings lives in the Zoom Account Management > Reports section. Look for Usage Reports, and then click Meeting to find the meeting you want, select the report type and date range, and generate the report.

Requirements: To generate an attendee list, you need to be the 1) the host of the meeting, 2) in a role with Usage Reports enabled, or 3) an account administrator or owner. You also need a Pro, API Partner, Business, or Education plan.

4. Collect Information From Attendees

In addition to getting an attendance sheet, you can also gather information from meeting attendees about themselves before they join the call. For example, you might want to require that attendees provide their name, company affiliation, or industry. To collect this information, first, you need to require Registration, an option found in the My Meetings tab of the Zoom web app. Then, you can set up a form that attendees must fill out before they can join the meeting. For the registration form, Zoom provides standard fields, such as name and company affiliation, that you add using checkboxes. To add new questions or fields, jump over to the tab called Custom Questions.

5. Record The Call As A Video

Zoom lets you record your web conferencing calls as videos, a handy feature for sharing the meeting with people who may have missed it, or for reviewing what was said. When you record, you must choose whether to use the local or cloud option. Local means you store the video file yourself, whether locally on your computer or in another storage space that you provide. With Cloud, which is for paying members only, Zoom stores the video for you in its cloud storage (different account types come with different amounts of storage). One convenience of the cloud option is that people can stream the video in a web browser once it's ready.

When creating a video from a conference call, it makes a big difference in the final quality to optimize a few settings in advance. For example, some calls might be broadcast-style, where only the host appears on the screen. In that case, set Zoom to only record the audio and video of the host. Other calls might be in the style of a collaborative meeting, in which case you want to record everyone. Be sure to explore Zoom's settings at least a few minutes before recording a call.

Requirements: To record videos, you need Zoom on macOS, Windows, or Linux. If you don't see the option to record, check your settings in the web app (under My Meeting Settings) or have your account administrator enable it. If you need to share the recording later, try one of these Zaps to automatically share once the recording has finished.

6. Have A Collaborative Annotation Session

Screen sharing allows the host of a call to display whatever's on their screen to everyone else on the call. Annotation tools let all the meeting participants draw and highlight what's on-screen, which can be immensely helpful when discussing visual materials, such as mockups, graphic designs, and so forth.

To annotate while viewing someone else's shared screen, select View Option from the top of the Zoom window, and then choose Annotate. A toolbar appears with all your options for annotating, including text, draw, arrow, and so forth. The presenter can use the save button on the toolbar to capture the complete image with annotations as a screenshot. You can also disable attendee annotation altogether.

7. Co-Host Calls

Meetings can have more than one person at the helm. A PR rep might want to cooperatively control a meeting alongside an executive, or a team with more than one lead may prefer to each co-host rather than choose one person over the other. Whatever your circumstances, you can start a Zoom call and have more than one person be in charge. To use co-hosting tools, you first must enable it in Zoom's Meeting Settings. Look for the Meeting tab and choose the Co-host option. Then, when you start a meeting, wait for your co-host to join, and add the person by clicking the three dots that appear when you hover over their video box. Alternatively, you can go to the Participants window, choose to Manage Participants, hover over the co-host's name, and select More to find the Make Co-Host option.

Requirements: To use co-hosting, you need a Pro, Business, Education, or API Partner account with Zoom, and you need to run on macOS, Windows, Android, or iOS (not Linux or web). If the option doesn't appear, ask your account administrator to enable the settings in the Meeting tab for co-hosting privileges.

8. Give Attendees A Waiting Room

Zoom lets attendees get into a video call with or without the host being present. Small groups sometimes like this option because they can have a few minutes to chit-chat before the meeting officially kicks off. In some situations, however, it could be in poor form to have attendees in a virtual room together, waiting for you to start. A better solution is to create a virtual waiting room, where attendees remain on hold until you let them in all at the same time or one by one. Precisely how you enable a waiting room depends on the type of account you have. When you set one up, however, you can customize what the attendees see while they await your grand entrance.

9. Let Someone Else Schedule Your Meetings

People who work with an assistant will love this option in Zoom that gives scheduling privileges to someone else. Whoever manages your calendar can now schedule Zoom calls for you. To set up the scheduling assistant privilege, log into Zoom, open Meeting Settings, and look under Other. You'll see a plus sign next to Assign Scheduling Privilege. Add your scheduling assistants by typing their email addresses and finish by clicking Assign. After you add your scheduling assistants, they must log out of Zoom and log back in for the feature to take effect. From this point on, assistants can create meetings for others by using the Schedule tool. Look for Advanced Options or Meeting Options (depending on which version of Zoom you use), and follow the prompts to create a new meeting.

Requirements: The primary Zoom account holder and everyone who receives scheduling privileges must all have Pro or

Corp licenses. And for webinars, both account holders and schedulers must have webinar licenses.

10. Learn A Few Essential Keyboard Shortcuts

If you use Zoom more than once a week, there are a couple of keyboard shortcuts worth learning to save you oodles of time.

I is for an invite. Press Cmd+I (macOS) or Alt+I (Windows) to jump to the Invite window, where you can grab the link to the meeting or send invitations to others via email.

M is for mute. Press Cmd+Ctrl+M (macOS) or Alt+M (Windows) when you are the meeting host and want to mute everyone else on the line.

S is for share. Press Cmd+Shift+S (macOS) or Alt+Shift+S (Windows) to share your screen

Advanced Tips And Tricks

Now the basics have been covered, there is a range of settings and features that more experienced users might want to use. Let's head back over to the web portal to run through a few options. If you are using the desktop application, you can quickly access this area by going to "Settings" -- > "View More Settings."

Under "Settings," Select "In Meeting: Advanced," To Find Features Including:

Breakout room: split meeting participants into separate, smaller rooms. This can also be done before a meeting begins to prevent logistics problems

Remote Support: allows a host to provide 1:1 support to a participant

Camera Control: you can allow a participant to take remote control of your camera

Show A "Join From Your Browser" Link: a workaround for users that can't download Zoom software

Invitation Languages: You can choose from a variety of languages for meeting invitations, including English, Spanish, French, and Russian.

Virtual Backgrounds: enabling/disabling

Waiting Room: a feature to keep participants in a 'waiting area' until the host is ready for them particularly handy for remote interviews or office hours. This feature is now on as default for education, Basic, and single-license Pro accounts.

10 Zoom Tips And Tricks You May Not Know

1. Virtual Background For Desktop And Mobile: This cool feature allows you to upload an image of anything you want your customer's logo or headquarters, a mountain scene, or professional office – to customize your background. It's available for both iPhones (8 and later) and desktops. At Zoomtopia we announced that by the end of this year, virtual backgrounds will no longer require a green screen on Mac devices!

2. Touch Up My Appearance: This instant filter provides a very subtle smoothing of fine lines and under-eye bags. It looks very natural – like you got a great night of sleep. How cool is that? To activate this feature, go to Settings, and under the Video tab, check the box next to Touch up my appearance.

3. Recording Transcripts: This option automatically transcribes the audio of a meeting or webinar that you record to the cloud. As the meeting host, you can edit your transcript. And when you share the recording, people can scan the text, search for keywords, click on any word in the transcript to access the video at that moment, or download the transcript.

4. 49 Person Gallery View: By turning on gallery view, you see up to 49 meeting participants at once, as opposed to the default 25, depending on your device.

5. Just For Admins: See all your users: Among our robust user management features, if you type a large number in the Page Size box to access all of your users. This will display all of your users on one page, and allow you to search for their names or update their departments easily.

6. Screen Sharing And Using Pause Share: You probably know you can easily share your whole screen or just an application, but did you know that you can pause your screen sharing? Simply press Pause Share when you don't want your fellow meeting participants to watch you fumble around with your presentation slides.

7. Share Computer Sound During Screen Sharing: Zoom screen sharing allows you to share the desktop, window, application, or audio/video. You can also send computer audio to the remote attendees when sharing a video or audio clip – no special plugins or cords needed. Sharing a video from Youtube has never been easier!

8. Wireless Screen Sharing With Zoom Rooms: Participants in Zoom Rooms can use one-click direct screen sharing from a Zoom desktop client on a Mac or Windows PC. Ultrasonic sound proximity detection enables the iPad controller to generate an ultrasonic signal that can be detected by the Zoom desktop client. If you don't have the Zoom client installed, just go to https://zoom.us/share and enter in a quick code. No cables or dongles needed.

9. Share And Annotate On Mobile: Share files directly from your phone while in the meeting and enjoy the whiteboarding feature on your phone, writing comments with your finger or stylus.

10. Multi-Share: Hosts using the Zoom desktop client can choose to allow multiple participants to share their screens simultaneously during a meeting. This can be useful for a real-time comparison of documents or other materials by participants in multiple locations. This is also available on Zoom Rooms.

Conclusion

Follow the guidelines and recommendations on securing Zoom. Keep all of the software on your computer updated and patched, not just Zoom. Use strong passwords, use two-factor authentication everywhere, to include Zoom, Google, Facebook, Twitter, etc. It's not like you don't have the time to figure it out now that you are stuck at home!

If you have a hard time figuring out how to secure all of your accounts, then set up a Zoom with a neighborhood teenager, your granddaughter, or your niece or nephew, and they will show you how. Most importantly, take every opportunity to connect with your friends, family members, neighbors, co-workers, and others in your community. It is clear that the human race is always stronger when we work together, we just need to re-envision what "together" looks like while we socially isolate to protect the most vulnerable in our society.

Zoom can be simple to use, but difficult to master. Even with these guides, take time to explore the app on your own, and discover everything it has to offer. With time, using Zoom to meet up with your colleagues will be as natural as meeting someone in real life. Zoom has become an essential tool for small-, medium-, and large-sized teams that want to keep in touch and continue their daily workflows with minimal disruption - as well as becoming a firm favorite with individuals. One way that teachers will be able to communicate with students during this school closure is to use Zoom.